Julia Roberts: A Cultural Phenomenon

Unveiling A Leading Star's Barrier-Breaking Career, Decades Of Success, Personal Life & Global Impact

Clarissa Morgan

All rights reserved. No part of this publication may be reproduced, distributed, or transmitted in any form or by any means, including photocopying, recording, or other electronic or mechanical methods, without the prior written permission of the publisher, except in the case of brief quotations embodied in critical reviews and certain other noncommercial uses permitted by copyright law.

© Clarissa Morgan, 2023.

Table of Content

Julia Roberts: A Cultural Phenomenon	0
Table of Content	2
Introduction	4
Chapter 1: Early Life and Family	**7**
Birth and Upbringing in Smyrna, Georgia	7
Education and Early Aspirations	9
Decision to Pursue Acting	11
Chapter 2: Breakthrough Roles	**14**
Mystic Pizza (1988) and Steel Magnolias (1989)	14
Rise to Stardom with Pretty Woman (1990)	17
Chapter 3: Decades of Success	**21**
Commercially Successful Films in the 1990s	21
Academy Award for Erin Brockovich (2000)	25
Chapter 4: Career Beyond the Big Screen	**29**
Television Roles and Achievements	29
Red Om Films Production Company	34
Chapter 5: Global Ambassador for Lancôme	**39**
Involvement with Lancôme since 2009	39
Impact on the Beauty Industry	44
Chapter 6: Financial Success and Recognition	**48**
Earnings and Net Worth	48
Accolades and People Magazine's "Most Beautiful Woman" Title	52
Chapter 7: Personal Life	**57**
Marriages and Relationships	57

    Family Dynamics and Personal Challenges   60
Chapter 8: Other Ventures and Interests   **67**
    Involvement in Philanthropy   67
Chapter 9: Legacy and Influence   **73**
    Julia Roberts' Lasting Impact on Hollywood   73
    Contributions to the Film and Entertainment Industry 79
Conclusion   **86**

Introduction

In the glittering expanse of Hollywood's illustrious history, one name shines as brightly as the stars that grace the silver screen—Julia Roberts. Born on October 28, 1967, in Smyrna, Georgia, this enigmatic actress has left an indelible mark on the world of cinema, capturing hearts and captivating audiences across the globe.

This introduction unveils the compelling journey of a girl with dreams as vast as the Southern skies, tracing the footsteps of Julia Fiona Roberts from her modest beginnings to the pinnacles of international stardom. As we navigate through the pages of her life, we encounter the pivotal moments that defined her ascent, from early breakthroughs in Mystic Pizza (1988) and Steel Magnolias (1989) to the iconic role that catapulted her into stardom—Vivian Ward in Pretty Woman (1990).

Beyond the cinematic allure, this narrative delves into Julia's multifaceted persona—exploring her roles as an actress, a producer through Red Om Films, and a global ambassador for Lancôme. We unravel the layers of her personal life, from tumultuous relationships to the profound impact of family dynamics, revealing the woman behind the silver screen.

Join me on a captivating odyssey through the life and legacy of Julia Roberts, a journey that transcends the frames of film and unveils the essence of an extraordinary individual who, with grace and talent, became not only Hollywood's most bankable star but a timeless icon etched in the annals of entertainment history.

Chapter 1: Early Life and Family

Birth and Upbringing in Smyrna, Georgia

The picturesque suburb of Smyrna, Georgia, welcomed Julia Fiona Roberts into the world on October 28, 1967, setting the stage for a life destined for cinematic greatness. Smyrna, a tranquil enclave just outside Atlanta, served as the backdrop to the earliest chapters of Julia's life. The crisp air and vibrant colors of autumn in Georgia became the canvas upon which the Roberts family's story began to unfold.

Born to Betty Lou Bredemus and Walter Grady Roberts, Julia's early days were marked by the warmth of a close-knit family in the Southern United States. Smyrna, with its community-oriented atmosphere, provided a nurturing environment for a young girl whose destiny would lead her far beyond the borders of this charming suburb. The cultural richness and hospitality of the South left an indelible mark on Julia's character, influencing her down-to-earth demeanor and endearing Southern charm.

Education and Early Aspirations

As Julia matured, her educational journey became an integral part of her formative years. Smyrna's educational institutions became the crucible where her academic and personal growth unfolded. Julia attended Fitzhugh Lee Elementary School, Griffin Middle School, and eventually Campbell High School. Each of these institutions not only imparted knowledge but also shaped the contours of her early aspirations.

From a young age, Julia's dreams were as expansive as the Southern skies. Her childhood ambition to become a veterinarian reflected a compassionate spirit and a love for animals. This early inclination hinted at a nurturing nature that would later manifest in her various roles, both on and off the screen.

Julia's participation in the school band, where she played the clarinet, showcased her artistic inclinations. Music became an early outlet for expression, foreshadowing her future in the creative arts. Despite the allure of music, the young Julia harbored a deeper passion—one that would lead her to the bright lights of Broadway and Hollywood.

Decision to Pursue Acting

Upon graduating from Smyrna's Campbell High School, Julia faced a pivotal crossroads. Her journey to self-discovery beckoned, and the allure of the performing arts proved irresistible. With an unwavering resolve, she made the life-altering decision to pursue a career in acting.

The transition from the serene landscapes of Smyrna to the bustling streets of New York City marked a significant chapter in Julia's life. Armed with determination and a fervent desire to make her mark in the world of entertainment, she signed with the Click Modeling Agency and immersed herself in acting classes. New York City, a melting pot of creativity and ambition, became the testing ground for Julia's aspirations.

In the city that never sleeps, Julia honed her craft, navigating auditions and refining her skills. The decision to pursue acting was not merely a career choice; it was a calling that resonated with her deepest aspirations. Julia's leap of faith into the competitive world of acting reflected her tenacity and unwavering belief in her abilities.

The challenges of the entertainment industry did not deter Julia. Instead, they fueled her determination to succeed. The early years in New York laid the foundation for a career that soon ascended to unparalleled heights. Julia's decision to embrace acting as her life's vocation marked the commencement of a journey that would captivate audiences worldwide.

Chapter 2: Breakthrough Roles

Mystic Pizza (1988) and Steel Magnolias (1989)

In the late 1980s, Julia Roberts' journey to cinematic stardom began with two pivotal roles that showcased her raw talent and foreshadowed the luminary career that lay ahead. "Mystic Pizza" (1988), a coming-of-age comedy-drama, marked Julia's initial foray into the world of film. Set in the quaint coastal town of Mystic, Connecticut, the film followed the lives of three young waitresses, including Julia's character, Daisy Araujo.

In "Mystic Pizza, " Julia's performance was a revelation. Her portrayal of Daisy, a headstrong and ambitious young woman navigating the complexities of love and friendship, resonated with audiences. Despite being an ensemble cast, Julia's on-screen charisma was undeniable, foreshadowing the star power that soon became her trademark.

Following the success of "Mystic Pizza, " Julia Roberts further solidified her presence in Hollywood with "Steel Magnolias" (1989). In this poignant drama-comedy, Julia starred alongside an ensemble cast featuring Sally Field, Dolly Parton, and Shirley MacLaine. The film, set in a small Southern town, explored themes of friendship, love, and loss, with Julia portraying Shelby Eatenton Latcherie, a character grappling with the complexities of life and motherhood.

Julia's performance in "Steel Magnolias" was met with critical acclaim, earning her a nomination for the Best Supporting Actress category at the Golden Globe Awards. These early roles not only showcased Julia's versatility but also set the stage for her meteoric rise in the film industry.

Rise to Stardom with Pretty Woman (1990)

The year 1990 marked a seismic shift in Julia Roberts' career, catapulting her to unprecedented heights of fame and acclaim. It was the year of "Pretty Woman, " a romantic comedy that not only defined an era but also etched Julia's name into the annals of Hollywood history. Directed by Garry Marshall, "Pretty Woman" paired Julia with Richard Gere, creating a cinematic chemistry that would captivate audiences worldwide.

In the film, Julia portrayed Vivian Ward, a vivacious and sharp-witted prostitute who, through a chance encounter, finds herself entangled in a whirlwind romance with a wealthy businessman, played by Gere. "Pretty Woman" was not merely a romantic comedy; it was a cultural phenomenon that resonated with audiences, transcending the conventional boundaries of the genre.

Julia's portrayal of Vivian was a revelation. Her infectious laughter, radiant charm, and the sheer authenticity she brought to the character elevated the film to unprecedented heights of success. Audiences were not just watching a love story unfold; they were witnessing the ascent of a star. Julia's performance earned her a nomination for the Academy Award for Best Actress, solidifying her status as one of Hollywood's leading ladies.

"Pretty Woman" not only dominated the box office but also became a cultural touchstone. Julia Roberts, with her megawatt smile and undeniable talent, became the embodiment of the modern romantic heroine. The film's success was a testament not only to the chemistry between its leads but also to Julia's ability to infuse depth and relatability into her characters.

The impact of "Pretty Woman" extended beyond its initial release. Julia Roberts became a household name, and her star power reached unprecedented levels. The film's iconic scenes, such as the shopping spree on Rodeo Drive and the fairy-tale ending on the fire escape, have become indelible moments in cinematic history. Julia's portrayal of Vivian Ward remains a defining moment in her career, a role that not only shaped the trajectory of her stardom but also left an enduring imprint on the romantic comedy genre.

Chapter 3: Decades of Success

Commercially Successful Films in the 1990s

As the curtains closed on the 1980s, Julia Roberts seamlessly transitioned into the next decade, etching her name in the golden pages of Hollywood's history. The 1990s proved to be a prolific era for the actress, marked by a string of commercially successful films that not only solidified her status as a bankable star but also showcased the breadth of her acting prowess.

One of the defining films of this era was "My Best Friend's Wedding" (1997), a romantic comedy that saw Julia in the role of Julianne Potter, a woman grappling with unrequited love. The film, directed by P. J. Hogan, not only resonated with audiences for its humor and heart but also showcased Julia's ability to navigate complex emotional terrain. Her performance was a testament to her versatility as an actress, further establishing her as the go-to leading lady for romantic comedies.

In 1999, Julia continued her streak of success with "Notting Hill. " Paired opposite Hugh Grant, she portrayed Anna

Scott, a glamorous movie star navigating the complexities of a relationship with an ordinary bookstore owner. The film's charm lay not only in its romantic narrative but also in Julia's ability to infuse authenticity and charisma into her character. "Notting Hill" reinforced her standing as the queen of romantic comedies, securing her place in the hearts of audiences around the world.

The same year brought "Runaway Bride, " a delightful romantic comedy reuniting Julia with her "Pretty Woman" co-star, Richard Gere. Directed by Garry Marshall, the film showcased the enduring chemistry between the two leads and further cemented Julia's reputation as the leading lady of choice for romantic comedies. The box office success of these films spoke volumes about Julia's star power and her ability to draw audiences into the enchanting worlds of love and laughter.

Beyond the romantic comedy genre, Julia Roberts demonstrated her versatility with "The Pelican Brief" (1993), a legal thriller in which she starred alongside Denzel Washington. The film, based on John Grisham's novel, showcased a different facet of Julia's acting prowess as she navigated the intricate world of conspiracy and legal intrigue.

However, the pinnacle of Julia's success in the 1990s undoubtedly came with her portrayal of the title character in "Erin Brockovich" (2000). While technically falling into the next decade, this film marked the culmination of Julia's dominance in the '90s and set the stage for a new chapter in her career.

Academy Award for Erin Brockovich (2000)

As the new millennium dawned, Julia Roberts entered the awards season with a performance that would not only redefine her career but also earn her the most coveted accolade in the film industry—the Academy Award for Best Actress. "Erin Brockovich," directed by Steven Soderbergh, was a biographical drama that brought to life the true story of Erin Brockovich, a legal assistant who spearheaded a legal battle against a major energy corporation accused of polluting a small town's water supply.

In this role, Julia Roberts transcended the confines of romantic comedies and showcased her dramatic range. Her portrayal of Erin Brockovich was a tour de force, characterized by a perfect balance of tenacity, vulnerability, and unyielding determination. Roberts immersed herself in the character, capturing the essence of a real-life woman who defied the odds and stood up for justice.

The impact of Julia's performance was immediate and profound. The film resonated with audiences, and critics lauded her transformative acting. When the Oscars night arrived in 2001, the world watched as Julia Roberts, with grace and humility, accepted the Academy Award for Best Actress. This moment marked not only a personal triumph for Julia but also a historic moment in Hollywood—an actress at the zenith of her career, receiving the industry's highest honor for her exceptional work.

The significance of "Erin Brockovich" extended beyond the awards and accolades. It signaled a paradigm shift in Julia Roberts' career, proving that she could seamlessly transition between genres and deliver performances that transcended the boundaries of romantic comedies. The film's success reaffirmed Julia's status as a powerhouse in the industry and opened new doors for her as a performer.

Chapter 4: Career Beyond the Big Screen

Television Roles and Achievements

As Julia Roberts' illustrious career unfolded on the silver screen, the actress took deliberate steps into the realm of television, expanding her artistic horizons and solidifying her status as a multifaceted talent. Beyond the cinematic glitz, Julia's venture into television showcased her ability to captivate audiences in the intimate confines of the small screen.

In 2014, Julia made a notable mark in television with her role in the HBO film "The Normal Heart. " Directed by Ryan Murphy, the film explored the early days of the AIDS crisis in New York City. Julia portrayed Dr. Emma Brookner, a character based on the real-life physician who was one of the earliest advocates for AIDS research. Her performance earned critical acclaim, and Julia received a Primetime Emmy Award nomination for Outstanding Supporting Actress in a Miniseries or a Movie.

This foray into television marked a significant shift for Julia, proving that her magnetic presence and acting prowess translated seamlessly from the big screen to the living rooms of viewers. "The Normal Heart" not only underscored Julia's commitment to compelling storytelling but also highlighted her willingness to engage with socially relevant and impactful narratives.

Building on this success, Julia Roberts ventured further into episodic television with the psychological thriller series "Homecoming. " Premiering on Amazon Prime Video in 2018, the series marked Julia's first regular television role. In "Homecoming, " she portrayed Heidi Bergman, a caseworker at a facility helping soldiers transition back to civilian life. The role allowed Julia to explore the complexities of her character over multiple episodes, showcasing her ability to sustain a character arc in the episodic format.

The critical acclaim for "Homecoming" solidified Julia's place in the evolving landscape of television. Her nuanced performance, coupled with the series' suspenseful narrative, demonstrated that Julia Roberts was not merely a film icon but also a force to be reckoned with in the episodic format. The series marked a new chapter in her career, reaffirming her relevance and versatility in an industry undergoing a paradigm shift with the rise of streaming platforms.

Expanding her television portfolio, Julia Roberts stepped into the world of political drama with the Starz limited series "Gaslit" in 2022. In this series, she portrayed Martha Mitchell, the wife of Attorney General John Mitchell, offering a nuanced portrayal of a woman caught in the tumultuous web of the Watergate scandal. The role once again showcased Julia's ability to bring depth and authenticity to historical characters, further enriching her television repertoire.

Julia Roberts' foray into television was not just about personal achievement; it also signified a broader trend in the entertainment industry. The migration of acclaimed actors to television underscored the changing dynamics of storytelling, with television becoming an increasingly attractive medium for exploring complex narratives and character arcs.

Red Om Films Production Company

Parallel to her acting career, Julia Roberts ventured into the realm of film production with the establishment of Red Om Films, a production company that would become a creative platform for the actress to shape and bring compelling stories to the screen. Founded in 1995, Red Om Films reflected Julia's commitment to fostering projects that resonated with her artistic sensibilities.

Under the banner of Red Om Films, Julia served as an executive producer for various projects, extending her influence beyond acting to the creative decision-making process behind the scenes. One notable collaboration was with director Steven Soderbergh on the film "Oceans Eleven" (2001). Julia not only starred in the film but also played a key role in its production, showcasing her ability to wear multiple hats in the filmmaking process.

Red Om Films also played a pivotal role in the American Girl franchise, producing the first four films from 2004 to 2008. These family-friendly films, inspired by the American Girl doll line, aimed to engage and inspire young audiences. Julia's involvement in these projects reflected her commitment to storytelling that had a positive impact on audiences, especially the younger generation.

Beyond film, Red Om Films extended its reach to the television landscape. The company collaborated with Lifetime to produce the television film "Mona Lisa Smile" (2003), a project in which Julia Roberts also starred. This expansion into television production marked a strategic move, aligning with the evolving trends in the entertainment industry and showcasing Julia's ability to navigate the shifting landscape.

As a production company, Red Om Films became a manifestation of Julia Roberts' vision for meaningful and impactful storytelling. It allowed her to champion projects that aligned with her values and offered a platform for diverse narratives. The company's involvement in both film and television demonstrated Julia's adaptability and foresight in navigating the evolving dynamics of the entertainment industry.

In addition to her work in front of the camera, Julia Roberts' role as an executive producer through Red Om Films contributed to shaping the narrative landscape. It underscored her commitment to stories that resonated with authenticity and social relevance, reflecting her influence not only as an actress but also as a creative force behind the scenes.

Chapter 5: Global Ambassador for Lancôme

Involvement with Lancôme since 2009

In 2009, the beauty industry witnessed a convergence of two influential forces—the timeless allure of Julia Roberts and the prestigious brand legacy of Lancôme. It was in this transformative year that Julia assumed the role of Global Ambassador for Lancôme, a partnership that not only redefined her relationship with the beauty industry but also leave an indelible mark on the perception of beauty and grace.

Lancôme, a French luxury cosmetics and skincare brand, has long been synonymous with elegance and sophistication. Julia Roberts, with her radiant smile and timeless beauty, seamlessly embodied the essence of the Lancôme woman. The collaboration was a marriage of iconic status and esteemed brand heritage, a perfect alignment that resonated with both the actress and the beauty powerhouse.

As the Global Ambassador, Julia Roberts became the face of Lancôme, representing the brand across the globe. Her association with Lancôme extended beyond the traditional role of a brand ambassador; it became a creative collaboration that allowed Julia to infuse her own personality and values into the brand's image.

One of the notable aspects of Julia's partnership with Lancôme was the authenticity she brought to the brand. In an era where the beauty industry often grapples with authenticity and relatability, Julia's approach to her role as Global Ambassador was refreshingly genuine. She was not just a face on a billboard; she became the embodiment of Lancôme's commitment to celebrating individuality and embracing the diverse expressions of beauty.

Julia's journey with Lancôme included the promotion of various iconic products, with a focus on Lancôme's skincare and makeup lines. From promoting groundbreaking skincare innovations to showcasing the timeless allure of Lancôme's iconic fragrances, Julia's influence permeated the brand's diverse product portfolio. Her involvement was not merely cosmetic; it was a narrative that unfolded through each campaign, capturing the essence of Lancôme's commitment to empowering individuals through beauty.

The collaboration with Lancôme also marked a significant moment in Julia Roberts' career trajectory. It showcased her ability to seamlessly transition between the realms of cinema and beauty, proving that her influence extended beyond the silver screen. As the Global Ambassador, Julia brought a sense of elegance, authenticity, and approachability to Lancôme, aligning the brand with values that transcended the superficial and resonated with a global audience.

Impact on the Beauty Industry

Julia Roberts' role as Global Ambassador for Lancôme reverberated far beyond the confines of advertising campaigns and glossy magazines. It had a profound impact on the beauty industry, redefining standards of beauty and challenging preconceived notions about age, grace, and individuality.

One of the notable contributions of Julia's collaboration with Lancôme was the celebration of ageless beauty. In an industry often criticized for its youth-centric ideals, Julia Roberts, in her 40s at the commencement of the partnership, became a symbol of timeless elegance. Lancôme's choice to have Julia as the face of the brand communicated a powerful message—that beauty knows no age limits. The actress's natural and radiant beauty became a beacon of empowerment for women of all ages, encouraging them to embrace their authentic selves with confidence.

The Lancôme campaigns featuring Julia Roberts were characterized by an emphasis on natural beauty and authenticity. Rather than conforming to conventional standards, the actress's images reflected a celebration of imperfections and individuality. This departure from the airbrushed perfection often associated with beauty campaigns resonated with consumers, fostering a sense of relatability and inclusivity.

Julia's impact on the beauty industry extended to the realm of skincare. Lancôme, under her influence, emphasized the importance of skincare as a journey rather than a destination. The actress's endorsement of Lancôme's skincare products communicated a message of self-care and embracing the aging process with grace. This narrative challenged the prevailing notion that beauty is solely about achieving an idealized image and instead focused on nurturing healthy and radiant skin at every stage of life.

Beyond the conventional beauty norms, Julia Roberts' collaboration with Lancôme championed the idea that beauty is a deeply personal and subjective experience. The actress's genuine and down-to-earth persona became synonymous with Lancôme's commitment to celebrating diversity and individual beauty journeys. This shift in perspective contributed to a broader industry conversation about redefining beauty standards and embracing a more inclusive definition of what it means to be beautiful.

Chapter 6: Financial Success and Recognition

Earnings and Net Worth

Julia Roberts, a name synonymous with Hollywood royalty, has not only left an indelible mark on the silver screen but has also carved her place among the highest-earning actresses in the industry. As one of the most bankable stars, Julia's financial success is a testament to her talent, business acumen, and enduring popularity.

Throughout her illustrious career, Julia Roberts has commanded substantial fees for her roles, setting records and paving the way for equitable compensation in the entertainment industry. Notably, in the late '90s and early 2000s, she reached unprecedented heights, becoming the world's highest-paid actress. Her groundbreaking fees for iconic roles, such as $20 million for "Erin Brockovich" (2000) and $25 million for "Mona Lisa Smile" (2003), reflected not only her star power but also the recognition of her exceptional contributions to the world of cinema.

The financial success of Julia Roberts is underscored by the sheer box office power of the films in which she has starred. Collectively, her films have grossed over $3. 9 billion globally, making her one of Hollywood's most lucrative assets. The romantic comedy "Pretty Woman" (1990), a cultural phenomenon in its own right, contributed significantly to this financial triumph, grossing over $463 million worldwide.

Beyond acting, Julia Roberts expanded her influence to film production through her production company, Red Om Films. While the financial details of the company's ventures may not be as widely publicized as her acting fees, the establishment of Red Om Films speaks to Julia's strategic approach to her career. As an executive producer, she not only added another dimension to her creative pursuits but also potentially participated in the financial success of the projects she championed.

As of 2020, Julia Roberts' net worth was estimated to be a staggering $250 million. This substantial financial portfolio is a culmination of decades of success, wise investments, and a keen understanding of the entertainment industry's dynamics. Julia's financial success extends beyond the glitz and glamour of Hollywood, positioning her as a shrewd and influential figure in the world of entertainment finance.

Accolades and People Magazine's "Most Beautiful Woman" Title

In the realm of accolades and recognition, Julia Roberts stands as a luminary with a mantle adorned with prestigious awards and titles. Her contributions to cinema have not only earned her critical acclaim but have also positioned her as a cultural icon, celebrated for both her talent and her enduring beauty.

One of the crowning achievements in Julia Roberts' career came with the pinnacle of recognition in the form of an Academy Award. In 2001, she clinched the coveted Oscar for Best Actress for her compelling portrayal of Erin Brockovich in the eponymous film. This accolade not only affirmed her acting prowess but also solidified her status among the Hollywood elite.

Beyond the Academy Awards, Julia Roberts has been the recipient of multiple accolades, including a British Academy Film Award and three Golden Globe Awards. Her ability to seamlessly transition between genres, from romantic comedies to dramatic roles, speaks to her versatility as an actress. These awards underscore not only her talent but also the universal appeal she brings to her diverse roles.

In the realm of beauty and glamour, Julia Roberts has graced the covers of numerous magazines, becoming a style icon and trendsetter. Her radiant smile and effortless elegance have made her a favorite among fashion enthusiasts and photographers alike. Notably, People magazine has bestowed upon her the title of the "Most Beautiful Woman in the World" a record five times. This recurring honor is a testament to Julia's timeless beauty and the enduring allure that captivates audiences around the globe.

The recognition of Julia Roberts as the "Most Beautiful Woman" extends beyond conventional standards of beauty. Her authenticity, grace, and approachability have played a pivotal role in reshaping perceptions of beauty in an industry often criticized for its narrow ideals. Julia's ability to embrace her natural self, including her famous megawatt smile, has resonated with audiences and contributed to her timeless appeal.

In addition to these prestigious accolades, Julia Roberts received a star on the

Hollywood Walk of Fame in 2000, further cementing her status as a Hollywood luminary. This recognition on the iconic Walk of Fame is a tribute to her enduring contributions to the entertainment industry and her lasting impact on popular culture.

Chapter 7: Personal Life

Marriages and Relationships

Beyond the glitz and glamour of Hollywood, Julia Roberts' personal life has been marked by a journey of love, relationships, and family. The actress, known for her captivating performances on screen, has also experienced the highs and lows of personal relationships, providing a glimpse into the complexities of her life beyond the movie sets.

Julia Roberts' romantic journey has been a subject of public fascination, and the actress has been open about the evolution of her relationships. In 1993, she married singer-songwriter Lyle Lovett in a surprise ceremony, capturing the attention of the media and fans alike. The marriage, however, was short-lived, and the couple divorced in 1995. Despite the brevity of their union, Julia and Lyle maintained an amicable relationship post-divorce, highlighting a mature approach to navigating the challenges of personal life in the public eye.

Following her divorce from Lovett, Julia Roberts found lasting love in cinematographer Daniel Moder. The couple tied the knot in 2002, and their union has endured the tests of time. Together, they have become parents to three children—twins Hazel and Phinnaeus, born in 2004, and son Henry, born in 2007. The family-oriented focus has been a cornerstone of Julia's personal life, and she has spoken about the joys and challenges of motherhood in various interviews.

In interviews, Julia has shared insights into the dynamics of her marriage and family. She emphasizes the importance of communication, mutual respect, and the ability to navigate challenges together. Despite the demands of their respective careers, Julia and Daniel have strived to create a supportive and nurturing environment for their children, balancing the responsibilities of parenthood with the demands of Hollywood.

Family Dynamics and Personal Challenges

The fabric of Julia Roberts' personal life is woven not only with the threads of romance but also with the intricate relationships within her family. Julia is the youngest of three siblings. Her older brother, Eric Roberts, and older sister, Lisa Roberts Gillan, are also actors. The dynamics of the Roberts family have been shaped by shared experiences in the world of entertainment, creating both bonds and, at times, challenges.

Julia's relationship with her brother Eric, in particular, has experienced periods of estrangement. The two siblings were reportedly estranged for several years until they reconciled in 2004. The complexities of familial relationships, coupled with the demands of their careers, led to a temporary rift that the siblings eventually overcame.

Lisa Roberts Gillan, Julia's older sister, has also pursued a career in acting. The shared passion for the arts within the family contributed to the establishment of a creative and supportive environment. Despite the challenges that can arise in the competitive world of entertainment, the Roberts siblings have demonstrated resilience and a commitment to familial bonds.

Tragedy struck the Roberts family with the loss of Julia's half-sister, Nancy Motes. Nancy, born to Julia's mother Betty Lou and stepfather Michael Motes, faced personal struggles that ultimately led to her untimely death at the age of 37 in 2014. The loss of a family member, added a layer of complexity to Julia's personal journey, underscoring the realities of both fame and the human experience.

In the realm of parental relationships, Julia Roberts' father, Walter Grady Roberts, passed away when she was just ten years old. The loss of a parent at a young age undoubtedly shaped Julia's perspective on family and resilience. Her mother, Betty Lou Bredemus, played a pivotal role in her upbringing.

Marriage and family life have not been without their challenges for Julia Roberts. Her mother, Betty Lou, filed for divorce in 1971, finalizing the separation in early 1972. Julia, then just a child, witnessed the complexities of adult relationships and the impact they can have on a family. Subsequently, Betty Lou married Michael Motes, a union that proved challenging, marked by issues of abuse and unemployment. The marriage ended in 1983, with Betty Lou citing cruelty as grounds for divorce.

The personal challenges Julia faced extended beyond family dynamics. In her early years, Roberts harbored dreams of becoming a veterinarian, a testament to her love for animals. However, life took a different turn, leading her to the path of acting. Despite not completing her education at Georgia State University,

Julia's decision to pursue a career in acting became a pivotal moment that shaped her destiny.

In 2014, Julia Roberts faced public scrutiny when her mother, Betty Lou, passed away at the age of 80. The loss of a parent is a profoundly personal experience, and Julia grieved while also contending with the intrusive nature of public attention during such intimate moments.

Despite these challenges, Julia Roberts' personal life has been a tapestry of resilience, love, and growth. Her journey reflects the universal themes of familial bonds, personal loss, and the intricate dance between public visibility and private struggles. Through it all, Julia has demonstrated a remarkable ability to navigate the complexities of her personal life with grace, embracing both the joys and tribulations that come with the human experience.

Chapter 8: Other Ventures and Interests

Involvement in Philanthropy

Julia Roberts is more than a Hollywood icon; she is a beacon of hope and change through her extensive involvement in philanthropy. Beyond the red carpet and cinematic brilliance, Roberts has passionately dedicated herself to causes close to her heart, channeling her fame and resources to make a meaningful impact on the world.

A cornerstone of Roberts' philanthropic journey is her role as a Goodwill Ambassador for UNICEF since 1995. Her commitment to the United Nations International Children's Emergency Fund has seen her actively championing the cause of children's rights and well-being. Through her travels to countries such as Haiti and India, she has shed light on the challenges faced by vulnerable children, advocating for their rights and mobilizing support for UNICEF's crucial initiatives.

Julia Roberts' philanthropic footprint extends beyond UNICEF. Her advocacy in the fight against cancer, a cause that became deeply personal following the loss of her father to the disease, led her to support organizations like Stand Up to Cancer. By lending her voice and influence, Roberts has contributed to collaborative efforts aimed at advancing cancer research and improving treatment outcomes.

Environmental conservation holds a special place in Julia Roberts' philanthropic portfolio. Her association with Earth Biofuels, a company dedicated to promoting environmentally friendly and sustainable energy solutions, showcases her commitment to addressing climate change. Roberts, through her involvement, advocates for the adoption of eco-friendly practices and raises awareness about the urgent need for sustainable energy alternatives.

Beyond global causes, Julia Roberts has extended her philanthropic arms to local communities. Her support for organizations working on education, women's rights, and poverty alleviation reflects a holistic approach to addressing societal challenges. Roberts actively engages with the communities and issues she supports, embodying the hands-on commitment that defines impactful philanthropy.

In 2017, Julia Roberts assumed the role of global ambassador for Community Organized Relief Effort (CORE), a non-profit organization founded by actor Sean Penn. CORE focuses on disaster response and community resilience, providing immediate relief in times of crisis. Roberts' involvement goes beyond fundraising; she actively participates in relief efforts during natural disasters, embodying a hands-on approach to humanitarian work.

The impact of Julia Roberts' philanthropy stretches beyond financial contributions. Her ability to leverage her celebrity status to bring attention to pressing issues has proven instrumental in garnering support and mobilizing resources. Roberts' advocacy is not a mere token gesture; it reflects a genuine commitment to creating positive change and addressing the root causes of social inequities.

Chapter 9: Legacy and Influence

Julia Roberts' Lasting Impact on Hollywood

Julia Roberts stands as a Hollywood luminary, leaving an indelible mark on the entertainment landscape that transcends the boundaries of time. Her legacy is not merely defined by box office successes or prestigious awards but is woven into the very fabric of Hollywood's narrative. Julia's enduring influence is a testament to her exceptional talent, versatile performances, and the profound impact she has had on both the film industry and popular culture.

One of the defining aspects of Julia Roberts' legacy is her ability to break barriers and redefine Hollywood norms. In an industry that often placed actresses in narrowly defined roles, Julia emerged as a trailblazer, challenging conventions and carving out spaces for women in cinema. Her breakthrough role in "Pretty Woman" (1990) not only catapulted her to stardom but also shattered preconceived notions about the kinds of characters women could portray on screen. Roberts' portrayal of Vivian Ward, a vivacious and empowered woman in a romantic comedy, became iconic and paved the way for a new era in female-led films.

Julia Roberts' legacy is intrinsically linked to her portrayal of strong, complex, and relatable female characters. Whether navigating the complexities of relationships in "My Best Friend's Wedding" (1997) or embodying the resilience of real-life figure Erin Brockovich in the eponymous film (2000), Roberts brought depth and authenticity to her roles. Her performances transcended the screen, resonating with audiences globally and influencing a generation of actors and filmmakers.

The cultural impact of Julia Roberts extends beyond her roles in individual films. She became a symbol of empowerment for women in the 1990s, a time when the industry was undergoing shifts in its portrayal of female characters. Roberts' characters were not defined solely by their relationships with men; they had agency, dreams, and narratives that went beyond traditional romantic storylines. Her influence in shaping a more inclusive and progressive Hollywood narrative cannot be overstated.

In addition to her groundbreaking roles, Julia Roberts' legacy is also marked by her status as a box office queen. The films in which she has starred collectively grossed over $3. 9 billion globally, making her one of the most commercially successful actresses in the history of cinema. Her ability to draw audiences to theaters became synonymous with success, solidifying her position as a bankable star.

Julia Roberts' impact on Hollywood is not confined to the 1990s; it has endured and evolved over the years. Her continued relevance in the 21st century speaks to the timeless quality of her performances and the enduring connection she maintains with audiences. Whether in ensemble heist films like "Ocean's Eleven" (2001) or in critically acclaimed dramas like "August: Osage County" (2013), Roberts continues to captivate viewers and contribute to the evolving landscape of cinema.

Beyond her individual achievements, Julia Roberts' legacy is intertwined with her role in reshaping the dynamics of gender and pay equity in the film industry. As one of the highest-paid actresses in the 1990s and early 2000s, she challenged the gender pay gap and set a precedent for advocating for equitable compensation. Her negotiations for substantial fees for roles like Erin Brockovich reflected a commitment to dismantling gender-based disparities in Hollywood.

Contributions to the Film and Entertainment Industry

Julia Roberts' contributions to the film and entertainment industry are both profound and multifaceted. Her influence extends beyond her performances to encompass her role as a producer, an advocate for change, and a cultural icon whose impact reverberates through various facets of the entertainment landscape.

As an actress, Julia Roberts' body of work is a testament to her versatility and range. From romantic comedies to intense dramas, she has navigated diverse genres with finesse, leaving an indelible mark on each. Her roles in iconic films like "Pretty Woman" (1990), "Erin Brockovich" (2000), and "Ocean's Eleven" (2001) showcase her ability to inhabit characters with depth and authenticity. Roberts' performances have set benchmarks for excellence, influencing a generation of actors and contributing to the evolving standards of cinematic storytelling.

Julia Roberts' foray into producing through her production company, Red

Om Films, reflects her commitment to shaping narratives and fostering new talent. As an executive producer, she played a pivotal role in bringing stories to the screen that resonated with her artistic sensibilities. Her involvement behind the scenes highlights a desire to contribute not only as an actress but also as a creative force shaping the industry's storytelling landscape.

Beyond her contributions to individual films, Julia Roberts has been an advocate for positive change within the film industry. Her stance on gender and pay equity has been instrumental in sparking conversations about the need for a more inclusive and equitable Hollywood. By negotiating substantial fees for her roles, she not only challenged established norms but also paved the way for a broader dialogue about fair compensation for actresses.

Julia Roberts' impact on Hollywood is also evident in her collaborations and ensemble casts. Her participation in films like "Ocean's Eleven" (2001) showcased her ability to seamlessly integrate into ensemble casts, contributing to the success of films driven by collective star power. These collaborations demonstrate her influence in creating cinematic experiences that go beyond individual performances.

As a cultural icon, Julia Roberts' influence extends to her role in shaping beauty standards and fashion trends. Her status as the "Most Beautiful Woman in the World" has not only made her a symbol of timeless elegance but has also contributed to redefining conventional notions of beauty in the industry. Roberts' presence on red carpets and magazine covers has set trends, emphasizing the importance of authenticity and confidence in the world of entertainment.

In the 21st century, Julia Roberts' contributions to the film industry have evolved with her embrace of television roles. Her venture into television with the psychological thriller series "Homecoming" (2018) and the political limited series "Gaslit" (2022) reflects a willingness to explore new avenues of storytelling. This transition underscores her adaptability and continued relevance in an industry experiencing transformative shifts in content consumption.

Julia Roberts' influence is not confined to the American film industry; it has a global resonance. Her films have achieved international acclaim, contributing to Hollywood's global appeal. Roberts' ability to connect with audiences transcends cultural boundaries, making her a global ambassador for the power of storytelling to foster understanding and empathy on a global scale.

Conclusion

In conclusion, this exploration of Julia Roberts' life, spanning her early years in Smyrna, Georgia, to her illustrious Hollywood career and multifaceted contributions, reveals a woman whose impact extends far beyond the silver screen.

Julia's journey, marked by breakthrough roles, decades of cinematic success, and a commitment to philanthropy, showcases the resilience, authenticity, and influence that define her legacy. From her timeless performances to her advocacy for gender equity and philanthropic endeavors, Julia Roberts has not only left an indelible mark on Hollywood but has also become a cultural icon whose influence transcends the boundaries of entertainment.

As we close this chapter on her life, it is evident that Julia Roberts' legacy is woven with talent, compassion, and a dedication to making a positive impact on the world, leaving an enduring imprint on the hearts of audiences globally.

Printed by Amazon Italia Logistica S.r.l.
Torrazza Piemonte (TO), Italy